CW00538612

8 contemporary pieces

for CLARINET and PIAN

UNBEATEN TRACKS

Edited by Paul Harris

CLARINET PART

FABER 𝆑𝆑 MUSIC

PREFACE

Contemporary music has always been the subject of controversy and strong feelings. However, in this important new collection of clarinet pieces you will find a treasure trove of fascinating music guaranteed only to delight and intrigue. As editor, my aim has been to add to our repertoire pieces that are stimulating and engaging, challenging, imaginative and tuneful – while remaining technically approachable. The composers have met this charge with consummate success.

There is much fun to be had in studying and performing these new pieces; I hope you enjoy playing them as much as I have! So, open the book and begin your voyage of discovery …

Paul Harris, March 2002

© 2002 by Faber Music Ltd
First published in 2002 by Faber Music Ltd
3 Queen Square London WC1N 3AU
Cover by Økvik Design
Music processed by Jackie Leigh
Printed in England by Caligraving Ltd
All rights reserved

ISBN 0-571-52003-0

To buy Faber Music publications or to find out about the full range of titles available please contact your local music retailer or Faber Music sales enquiries:
Faber Music Ltd, Burnt Mill, Elizabeth Way, Harlow CM20 2HX
Tel: +44 (0)1279 82 89 82   Fax: +44 (0)1279 82 89 83
sales@fabermusic.com   www.fabermusic.com

To Elsa Verdehr

Reef Singing

Peter Sculthorpe

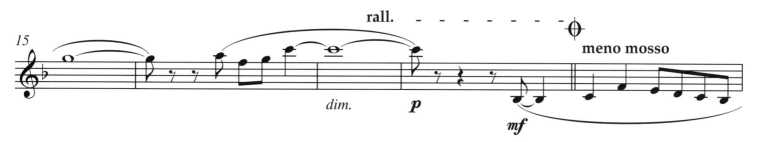

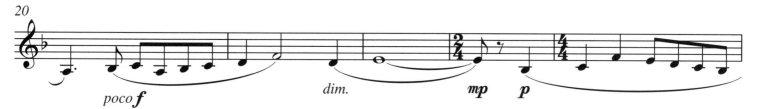

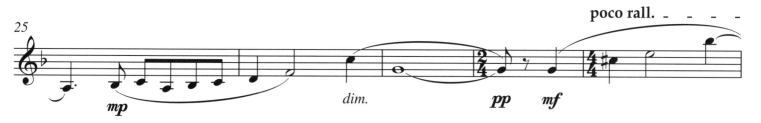

Lower Ground

Lloyd Moore

Reluctant Ragtime

Christopher Gunning

Elegiac Waltz

Eddie McGuire

March

Huw Watkins

Night Run

John Hawkins

Clay

Edward Rushton

Escapology

Richard Harris

8 contemporary pieces

for CLARINET and PIANO

UNBEATEN TRACKS

Edited by Paul Harris

© 2002 by Faber Music Ltd
First published in 2002 by Faber Music Ltd
3 Queen Square London WC1N 3AU
Cover by Økvik Design
Music processed by Jackie Leigh
Printed in England by Caligraving Ltd
All rights reserved

ISBN 0-571-52003-0

To buy Faber Music publications or to find out about the
full range of titles available please contact your local music
retailer or Faber Music sales enquiries:

Faber Music Ltd, Burnt Mill, Elizabeth Way, Harlow CM20 2HX
Tel: +44 (0)1279 82 89 82   Fax: +44 (0)1279 82 89 83
sales@fabermusic.com   www.fabermusic.com

FABER *ff* MUSIC

PREFACE

Contemporary music has always been the subject of controversy and strong feelings. However, in this important new collection of clarinet pieces you will find a treasure trove of fascinating music guaranteed only to delight and intrigue. As editor, my aim has been to add to our repertoire pieces that are stimulating and engaging, challenging, imaginative and tuneful – while remaining technically approachable. The composers have met this charge with consummate success.

There is much fun to be had in studying and performing these new pieces; I hope you enjoy playing them as much as I have! So, open the book and begin your voyage of discovery …

Paul Harris, March 2002

COMPOSER BIOPICS

All contributing composers were asked to give their own personal responses to the following questions; of course their answers can only reflect their views now and will be ever-changing:

Date and place of birth

Musical works that have most inspired you

Individuals who have most inspired you

What your piece means to you

A quote that you feel best describes your music in general

Your two favourite books

CHRISTOPHER GUNNING

Date and place of birth	05.08.44 Cheltenham.
Inspiring musical works	Symphony No 7, Jean Sibelius; *Porgy and Bess*, George Gershwin arr. for Miles Davis by Gil Evans; *Daphnis et Chloé*, Maurice Ravel; Symphony No 3, Witold Lutoslawski; *Das Lied von der Erde*, Gustav Mahler.
Inspiring individuals	Brian Trowell; Dudley Moore; Richard Rodney Bennett.
What your piece means to you	My daughter Chlöe has often been reluctant to practise her clarinet, but once she's started, usually enjoys herself. This piece is like that – tentative at first, but becoming more enthusiastic.
A quote	I like to portray emotions and characters in music, and that partly explains why I have been drawn towards composing music for films and television. The twentieth century has provided me with a fantastic variety of idioms in which to work, and though I have no hesitation in using whatever methods feel appropriate, I always try to find the most direct and simple way of achieving the desired result.
Two favourite books	*The Damp Garden*, Beth Chatto; Collected Poems (especially 'The Love Song of J Alfred Prufrock' and 'The Waste Land'), T S Eliot.

RICHARD HARRIS

Date and place of birth	05.03.68 Kent.
Inspiring musical works	Violin Concerto in D, Johannes Brahms; *Romeo and Juliet*, Sergey Prokofiev; 'Neptune' from *The Planets*, Gustav Holst; Kenny Kirkland's jazz piano solo on the live album *Bring On the Night*, Sting.
Inspiring individuals	Charles Darwin; Branford Marsalis; Dave Holland; Sachin Tendulkar.
What your piece means to you	The opening theme started life in an unfinished viola piece ten years ago. I am very happy to have presented a piece that feels simultaneously immediate and yet ten years in the making; and the title reflects the twists and turns of the compositional journey!
A quote	Music that needs writing about is like architecture that needs dancing about.
Two favourite books	*Your Face Here – British cult movies since the Sixties*, Ali Catterall and Simon Wells; *To Kill a Mockingbird*, Harper Lee.

JOHN HAWKINS

Date and place of birth	16.01.49 London.
Inspiring musical works	Never admit your sources, as the ones that help the most are not necessarily the best!
Inspiring individuals	Mark Twain (a melancholy man who managed not to take himself too seriously and write a lot); anyone who can mend cars.
What your piece means to you	Frightened exchanges across some dark, urban frontier?
A quote	'Everything should be made as simple as possible – but no simpler.' (Anonymous)
Two favourite books	*Le Petit Prince*, Antoine de Saint-Exupery; *Catch-22*, Joseph L Heller.

EDDIE McGUIRE

Date and place of birth	15.02.48 Glasgow.
Inspiring musical works	When I was 13: *Syrinx*, Claude Debussy. When I was 30: *Music for 18 Musicians*, Steve Reich. Always: Clarinet Concerto in A, Wolfgang Amadeus Mozart.
Inspiring individuals	John Cage (and his leaps of imagination).
What your piece means to you	The melodic material carries the feeling that life must go on, even after tragic events – that of striving for a better world. The piece was completed in August 2001 when my focus was on the Middle East; the following month much worse was to happen. Using a dance form as a lament may seem contradictory but I feel the flow of the waltz adds much-needed optimism.
A quote	'It is great to hear McGuire in this mode, grasping the sterile techniques of minimalism and tone rows, warming them with the flash of invention. Let's hear more.' (Mary Miller, *The Scotsman*)
Two favourite books	*Wide Sargasso Sea*, Jean Rhys; *River out of Eden*, Richard Dawkins.

LLOYD MOORE

Date and place of birth	19.02.66 London.
Inspiring musical works	*Symphonie fantastique*, Hector Berlioz; *La Mer*, Claude Debussy; Symphony No 6, Gustav Mahler; *Tapiola*, Jean Sibelius.
Inspiring individuals	Edgard Varèse; Benjamin Britten.
What your piece means to you	I have tried to create a 'mood' piece that gets the maximum out of the minimum of resources – the challenge was to write something interesting to play and listen to, within this quite limited framework.
A quote	'Music bursting with things to say.' (*The Sunday Times*)
Two favourite books	*Crime and Punishment*, Fyodor Dostoyevsky; *A History of the World in 10 ½ Chapters*, Julian Barnes.

EDWARD RUSHTON

Date and place of birth	10.12.72 Norwich.
Inspiring musical works	*The Consolations of Scholarship*, Judith Weir; Third Concerto for Orchestra, Robin Holloway; *The Carla Bley Big Band Goes to Church*, Carla Bley; *The Confession of Isobel Gowdie*, James MacMillan; *Three Screaming Popes*, Mark-Anthony Turnage.
Inspiring individuals	Hector Berlioz; Will Humburg (German conductor and my former boss); William Coleman (English singer and friend); my wife Dagny Gioulami and my daughter, Emily Lola.
What your piece means to you	It's like a fragment of pottery found at an archaeological site, affording a glimpse into a lost civilisation; strange and distant, yet whimsical and attractive.
A quote	My teacher Robin Holloway once wrote, about a piece that I'd written: 'Wholly individual and strange'. I would love this to be something that could be applied to my music as a whole!
Two favourite books	*The Unconsoled*, Kazuo Ishiguro; *Skipped Parts*, Tim Sandlin.

PETER SCULTHORPE

Date and place of birth	29.04.29 Launceston, Tasmania.
Inspiring musical works	Australian aboriginal music, Japanese court music, Balinese Gamelan music and plainsong.
Inspiring individuals	The writer, Patrick White; the painter, Russell Drysdale; the architect, Andrea Palladio.
What your piece means to you	When I play the piece on the piano, thoughts of Australia's Top End come into my mind. In particular, I think of the area from the city of Darwin to the islands of Torres Strait, at Australia's northern-most tip. This is one of my favourite parts of the world, a place of endless summer.
A quote	In the programme note to my orchestral work *Earth Cry*, I wrote that we in Australia '… need to attune ourselves to this continent, to listen to the cry of the earth, as the Aborigines have done for many thousands of years'. This belief lies at the heart of almost all my music.
Two favourite books	*The first discovery of Australia and New Guinea*, George Collingridge; *Lord Jim*, Joseph Conrad.

HUW WATKINS

Date and place of birth	13.07.76 Pontypool, Wales
Inspiring musical works	Piano Quartets in G minor and E♭ major, Wolfgang Amadeus Mozart; *Curlew River*, Benjamin Britten; Duo for violin and piano, Elliott Carter; Two Songs, Op.91, for contralto, viola and piano, Johannes Brahms.
Inspiring individuals	Musically and compositionally: Julian Anderson.
What your piece means to you	I wanted to write a piece that was made rhythmically more irregular than the time signature of 4/4 would suggest. It is not a straightforward March!
A quote	'[The nineties was a period in which] a young talent such as Huw Watkins, emerging from an entirely classical background, could still engage his listeners, not out of some cute mix of current styles, but through the cogency of his compositional invention.' (Bayon Northcott, *The Independent*)
Two favourite books	*The Magus*, John Fowles; *If on a Winter's Night a Traveller*, Italo Calvino

To Elsa Verdehr

Reef Singing

Peter Sculthorpe

Lower Ground

Lloyd Moore

18
21
f molto espr.
24
ff
mp
p
28
ad lib., senza misura
rall.
colla parte

Reluctant Ragtime

Christopher Gunning

Elegiac Waltz

Eddie McGuire

18

March

Huw Watkins

Night Run

John Hawkins

Clay

Edward Rushton

Escapology

Richard Harris